FROM THE ANDES TO VANCOUVER

A STAND FOR JUSTICE

www.mascotbooks.com

From the Andes to Vancouver: A Stand for Justice

For more information, please contact:
Mascot Books
620 Herndon Parkway, Suite 320
Herndon, VA 20170
info@mascotbooks.com

Library of Congress Control Number: 2018915237

CPSIA Code: PRV0919A
ISBN-13: 978-1-64307-434-4

Printed in the United States

For Manuel

PROLOGUE

Before the Spanish conquistadors invaded what is now called South America, there was another civilization that stretched out over the western half of the continent. The natives called this nation "Tawantinsuyo"—or "the four regions"—but it became known to the world as the Inca Empire.

Tawantinsuyo was a monarchy, ruled by the Inca ("Inca" simply means "ruler" in the native Quechua language). As with all monarchies, the ruler would offer protection to his people with his army, and in exchange, the citizens would pay tribute in the form of *mit'a*—mandatory public service required of every family.

In 1532, the Inca were attacked by the rapidly expanding Spanish Empire. After finding gold and silver in the Andes, they moved like men possessed by evil forces, claiming ownership of every new place they encountered. Like a wildfire, the Spanish devoured anything and everything. The timing was also on the side of the Spanish conquerors because the Incas were divided between two brothers. Also, the conquerors unwittingly brought with them other tools of devastation: the chickenpox and measles viruses. These diseases ravaged the native population. By 1572, the last Inca resistance ended; their rudimentary weapons were no match for the firepower of Spain.

The conquistadors had become especially interested in Alto Peru (now known as Bolivia) because of the immense amount of silver found there. *Mit'a* became "la mita"—a means to enslave the natives and exploit their labor in the silver mines. Spanish greed for silver had no limits; by the early 17th century, the small mining town of Potosi, Bolivia would become the fourth most populated city in the world. Some have said there was enough silver found in Bolivia to build a bridge all the way to Madrid, and just beside it, another bridge with the bodies of all the Indians that died for this cause. The Spaniards even brought ships filled with African slaves to work the silver mines, but the drastic change in climate and altitude caused many of them to die. A Catholic monk convinced the conquistadors that it was useless to keep them in Potosi, and took them to the more tropical Yungas, Bolivia.

Now the only alternative the Spanish conquerors saw was to enslave as many natives as they could get ahold of.

There were several attempts by the natives to retake control of their lands. Even though none were successful, one of these fights stood out for its intensity and cruelty: In 1781 a merchant named Julian Apaza Nina, disgusted with the treatment of his people, decided to prompt a rebellion against Spanish rule. He adopted the name Tupac Katari in honor of two previous indigenous leaders who were executed by the Spanish.

Together with his wife Bartolina Sisa—who was a great warrior herself—and other native leaders, he gathered 40,000 men willing to fight against the Spanish Crown. Katari and his men attempted to siege the city of La Paz twice; in both instances they were soundly defeated. The Spanish army decided to make sure that no more insurgencies would occur. They executed Tupac Katari by dismemberment at a public plaza, in front of his horrified people, with four horses pulling him apart. Each part of his body was sent to the far reaches of Alto Peru and exposed to the general public. The Spanish wanted people to see his remains, and know who was in power. Tupac Katari's final words were, "I will return and I will be millions!"

These failed rebellions shattered the spirit of the *indios*. Even though soon after these events, Bolivia became an independent country, the *indios* entered a dark age that would last nearly two more centuries. They would be promised freedom, only to see it be taken away again and their position exploited by those in power. During this time, there was much more bloodshed on all sides. The natives lived and died with their dignity trampled over and over. The only options available to them were slavery, or to be so underpaid that it kept them in a vicious cycle of deep poverty and ignorance. Some natives refused to accept these choices and fled into the mountains where they settled and formed their own communities. Life in these arid places was difficult, but—to the *indios* who chose it—it was a fair price to pay for freedom.

The natives' lives had been upended by this state of affairs. They had ruled their own land and reaped its natural bounty; now they were utterly subjugated by the Spanish. Their self-esteem was destroyed. They were mocked and humiliated in terrible ways, and made to be the victims of crimes that went unpunished. For the Spanish rulers, these *indios* were mindless beasts of burden.

The *indios* lived believing they were an inferior race: the whites were the *patrones* ("bosses") and the natives were their servants.

As history unfolded, there were other changes in Upper Peru. Some Spanish men had children with native women; their offspring were called *Mestizos* ("mixed"). The children of pure Spanish families born in South America were called *Criollos*. These were some of the new castes—or levels—forming in Latin American society. The natives had always been treated as an inferior race, but now the Mestizos and even the Criollos were likewise placed below the Spanish. Eventually the majority non-Spanish populace rose up and threw off the shackles of their oppressors. In 1809, a rebellion in Upper Peru marked the "first cry of freedom" in Latin America; 16 years later, the fighters proclaimed the free Republic of Bolivia.

But the *indios'* work for true freedom was far from over. Even though Bolivia's Constitution was founded in equality and justice for all, it would still be a long struggle before the many peoples that made up Bolivia could live in harmony...

I

THE CHILD

1940
Rosario Provincia Pacajes, La Paz, Bolivia

A several hours drive from La Paz city, further into the Andes, there is a small village called Rosario. In those days, the village's population was at most a hundred people. Surrounded by mountains, and at 13,000 feet above sea level, oxygen is scarce here. Because it is so close to the sun, an overwhelming brightness permeates everything. The atmosphere is extremely cold. The wind howls through the mountains. These conditions create a very unfriendly environment for living creatures. The plant life is limited to cactus-like shrubs, quinoa, and potatoes. The fauna is also scarce: vicuña, armadillo, and the Andean condor live in the wild while cows, sheep, and llamas are kept for farming. This village was a refuge to the *indios*. Due to its hostile environment, the *patrones* didn't venture here; native families lived more or less at peace, but somewhat disconnected from the rest of the country.

It was a Saturday morning. Everyone in the village was gathered at their community church. All eyes followed the pastor as he walked across the room and fervently read one of the Psalms:

"The Lord reigns, let the earth be glad; let the distant shores rejoice!

Clouds and thick darkness surround Him; righteousness and justice are the foundation of His throne.

Fire goes before Him and consumes His foes on every side.

His lightning lights up the world!"

Then the pastor looked at everyone and spoke.

"Dearly beloved...God is almighty. He loves good, and hates evil. We humans, because of our sins, alone, could never look to Him, never deserve His love. But He loves us, with all His heart. He made each one of us unique, and yet alike in His image. Mankind is lost in worldly things, but He does not want to lose us. That's why He sent us Jesus, so that Jesus—as the perfect man—would be sacrificed and used as God's Lamb, to wash away our sins!"

At the very first row of seats there was a family with seven children, listening carefully to the pastor.

The youngest of all was a seven-year-old child who was trying very hard to understand the sermon. Totally in awe, believing every word about this wonderful God that loves mankind to the point that He would die for us....the pastor's words would stay in his head forever.

A few days later the boy, whose name was Constantino, was hopping along one of the mountain paths that led to his tiny home. It was very early in the morning, and very cold—yet, he didn't seem to mind the frigid temperatures and howling wind; he was filled with joy, the kind that only children feel. Ambrosia, his mother, was going to take him to the *mercado* for the first

time, and he was excited! The *mercado* was in a town further towards La Paz city. There, on Wednesdays and Saturdays, people went to trade all kinds of goods. She made a wordless sign to Constantino to start heading toward the road. She was trying not to wake the rest of the family.

Ambrosia was selling dry wood. She had a couple of bundles that she was going to load onto the truck that would transport them.

They were both dressed in the typical clothing of that time. Everything was hand woven from sheep and llama wool. Constantino wore a hand-knitted hat that covered his ears and sported llama patterns like those on his sweater. His pants were slightly small on him, and his shoes were beaten and worn. His mother wore a long *pollera* (long native typical skirt) and a thick, knitted sweater. Two long braids of shiny, silky black hair adorned her face. Their bronze skin was weather-beaten, their cheeks burgundy red from the extreme cold and burning sun, and they bore pearly sets of white teeth (they never ate sugar).

After a four-hour ride, the truck left them at the busy town called Ayo-Ayo.

Ambrosia walked fast, and little Constantino tagged along. She wanted to get an early start so that they could get back home in time to prepare dinner, but Constantino kept getting distracted. He found everything so interesting, so many things that he had never seen! At one point, he pulled on his mother's sleeve, and in a very soft voice asked, "Who are all these people, Mommy? They are so white. Why are we different?"

"They are the *patrones*, my son."

The answer he got from his mother was confusing. He was expecting some further explanation, but she didn't seem to think it was necessary.

The day went on, and the sales were good. Soon it was time to go home. They had just one more stop at a lady's house, for a payment. Just as they were about to knock on the door, two big black dogs attacked Ambrosia and bit her leg! Constantino and his mother defended themselves the best they could, and in a couple of minutes the dogs backed away, continuing to bark from a short distance. Two young Spanish men opened the door, looked at Constantino and his mother, then began to call to their own mother: "Mom! Come! These stupid *indios* kicked our dogs!"

A woman stepped out of the house. She seemed very upset and called the dogs inside. She looked at Constantino's mother. The wound on her leg was bleeding, and Ambrosia's face wracked with pain, but the woman didn't care. She sounded impatient when she spoke.

"Well, you should be careful! Do not kick my dogs! Here, take your money and go home! You'll be fine." Then she forced the money into Ambrosia's hand, walked back over her porch, and slammed the door.

But Ambrosia wasn't fine. She was crying in pain, so she and Constantino went to the police to ask for help.

The police didn't care either. They didn't help at all; in fact, they demanded that the two *indios* leave right away. They also recommended that Ambrosia never mess with the *patrones*—and to make things worse, as they were leaving the station, a *patron* himself gave a push and a kick to Ambrosia because she was taking too long!

This was the first time that Constantino saw the reality of life for native people. He tried so hard to understand what was going on. Why, instead of anyone trying to help them, did it seem that everyone was bothered by their presence? Did they do something that offended somebody? He and his mother were humiliated by these white people! He felt anger rapidly growing in his chest. It wasn't just the fact that the police hadn't said a word to the white woman, or even that the dogs had been so vicious. It was the expressions on their faces that bothered him the most, as if they were "things"—smelly and filthy, and not even worth anyone's time. *And why did Mother let them get away with it?* he thought. *What kind of injustice is this, that people demand respect, but they don't give any respect to us?*

On their way home, Constantino looked up at his mother and asked, "Who were those people? How are we different? Why were they so *mean?*"

The response he got was a simple shrug.

"That's just how it is."

When the truck stopped at their village, Constantino quickly jumped off and ran to his house. His eyes were red, with thick tears rolling down his cheeks. His chest was beating almost out of control. He slammed the front door behind him and hurried to his father Manuel's arms, dropping to his knees as he choked and told him what happened. Manuel cried with him, but soon calmed him down. Ambrosia joined them too.

Manuel, who was a devoted student during his spare time, gathered the rest of his family and explained the entire political situation to them as he took out an old illustration of a world map.

"The white men come from Spain. Their land is across the sea. They came here in search of our silver. They don't think like us. Their concern is for money and power. To them, our lives are worthless. We *indios* have lived here for thousands of years. Our ancestors reaped the fruit of this land and lived off of its great wealth without resorting to such greed, but times are different now."

Then Manuel told his family the story of Tupac Katari and his wife Bartolina. He advised them to study with all their strength, to dream of a better future, and to become successful for the sake of their people. He said knowledge was the most powerful weapon against oppression.

Constantino paid close attention to his father's wise words. Since school was several miles away, he had to be patient and wait until he was old enough to make the journey alone. At age 13, he enrolled in first grade. He immediately took to learning. He excelled in every subject, especially in social studies. Many times he went far beyond what teachers assigned for homework. He amazed everyone. They even let him skip a grade.

Soon the time came for Constantino to attend middle school, which was much further away. Financial help came from his local Seventh Day Adventist church, which had connections all over Bolivia. Seeing that Constantino was an excellent student, the church agreed to help him go to Cochabamba, where they had a school of their own and he would not have to pay tuition!

And so he left his tiny village, alone, with only a few coins in his pocket, and the best clothes from his humble wardrobe. The road to Cochabamba was long. At first, the trail was rocky and full of dust, but after a few hours he could feel the air getting warmer and becoming more pleasant. It was very different than La Paz.

Cochabamba is a peaceful valley filled with various trees, flowers, and all types of vegetation. For most of the year, the valley is a temperate 72 degrees. Some parts of the road are even adorned with beautiful palm trees. There is a reason that Cochabamba has a second name: "The Eternal Spring."

Venturing farther from his home helped Constantino become more aware of the plight of his fellow natives. He had a firsthand view of discrimination everywhere. After several years of school, when he was about 18 years old and on the cusp of manhood, he was brimming with energy and confidence. This made him more daring when he saw the mistreatment of his people. Many times he got into fistfights trying to defend them. He was constantly bullied by the whites and half-whites. All of this could have broken Constantino, but instead it made him stronger, made him love his people more. It gave him a reason to study harder and think about the better future his father spoke of. There were many sleepless nights when the last words of Tupac Katari would ring in his head: "*I will return as millions!*"

Walking through the streets, all he saw was white men in control and *indios* serving them. His own people seemed to be unwilling to change this. Natives had lost all faith in themselves; their spirits seemed to be utterly defeated. After a lot of thinking, he came to the conclusion that the very first step to free his people from oppression was to make them believe in themselves again. But how?

There were times during school breaks that he would travel back to his home village, Rosario. His favorite part of being home—besides the love of his family—was the majesty of the Andes. He especially enjoyed running along the path from his home to the top of a nearby mountain. He would race his shadow all the way up and finally, once there, totally out of breath, stop and admire the beauty of his homeland. There he felt totally connected with nature. Native people deeply believe in the unity of all living things, and they embrace Mother Earth.

At the top of that mountain, barely a quarter mile from his home, while he waited to see an Andean Condor pass by, a gust of wind would hit his body and nearly lift him off the ground. This was when Constantino felt that oneness: he was this mountain, these rivers, those far away trees, and the strong winds that could carry his spirit to endless places. This was home, and he loved it.

He knew that the key to freeing native people must involve better access to education. This would allow natives to understand the system imposed on them by the *patrones*—and perhaps enable them to stop living in fear. Constantino would weep when he thought of how his people were destined to suffer if they didn't stand up for themselves. He knew he needed to do something, and it had to be big enough to change the course of Bolivia's history, but he also knew he couldn't do this alone.

II

GETTING TO KNOW HIS STRENGTHS

Constantino's education was put on hold at age 19. Like every Bolivian male at that age, he was required to undertake mandatory military service. He returned to La Paz, where there was another small town: Viacha. Constantino saw this as a great opportunity to develop survival skills. His father had already taught him to be fit, healthy, and strong,  but this new experience was going to prove very handy indeed.

The training for soldiers was intense. Constantino enjoyed the challenges, in large part because he always seemed to do better than most of the other trainees.

The year Constantino was conscripted, 1952, was the year of the Bolivian National Revolution. His orders were to subdue the insurgents, even though his heart was with them and their cause. For the insurgents wished for universal votes and access to universities, which he also wanted, but he could not say so as a conscripted member of the military.

One experience taught Constantino a valuable lesson about controlling his fear. He and a few other soldiers were holed up in a building, surrounded by revolutionaries. Suddenly, a mortar shell landed just a few feet away from them! Constantino quickly jumped from the second floor, using the butt of his rifle to break his fall. He was being shot at from all directions—several bullets ended up in his body—but he ran for his life and eventually made it to safety. He now knew that his life depended on mastering and overcoming his fears. Being in the military service also helped him develop many more survival and fighting skills. Little did he know how handy all these things would soon be to him.

But just after completing his time in the military, Constantino needed to go back home. His mother was dying. At her bedside, he remembered that day at the *mercado*. He wept in pain and burned with anger. He wished nobody had disrespected her like that. He wished he could change that memory.

After mourning for his mother, Constantino traveled to La Paz City, the epicenter of Bolivia. He decided to continue high school there. Eventually he would attend the country's most well-known university, *Universidad Mayor de San Andrés* (UMSA).

As always, the trip from Rosario was treacherous. The bus Constantino took was filled to at least twice its normal capacity. It creaked and shuddered through the winding mountain roads, constantly being pelted by wind and gravel. The old bus moved slowly but steadily toward the big city

As the bus inched closer to La Paz, Constantino smiled and breathed deeply. He looked out the window at the great Illimani, the second highest mountain in Bolivia. He struggled to train his eyes on its peak, for it rose above the clouds and beyond the sight of anyone on the ground.

Constantino looked ahead: they should have been nearing La Paz by now. Instead, what he saw was a line of cars appearing to sink below the horizon. As the bus got closer, he noticed that the road became extremely steep—the cars and buses were forced to inch down this road at a snail's pace. Constantino had heard about La Paz lying inside a great bowl-shaped valley, protected from the harsh weather of the surrounding Andes. When his bus finally arrived in the city, he saw a teeming labyrinth of narrow, busy streets. Colonial Spanish architecture was interspersed with square, modern buildings that impressed Constantino deeply. Most magnificent of all was the university itself, which cast a shadow over everything around it.

Once he established himself in the city, Constantino looked for a job. Trying to settle into life in La Paz was a long, arduous process. He found a job at a glass shop and tried to focus on finishing his secondary schooling so that he could apply to the university. The years went by, and Constantino found success as a glass cutter—he even got his own shop to run! This allowed him to buy his own house and live somewhat comfortably. He had heard that a few *indios* were being admitted to UMSA, and was eager to join them and learn more about political science. Finally, the day came when he was admitted to the university.

On the first day of classes, Constantino entered a classroom and saw a sea of white and half-white young men. He tried not to draw attention to himself, but it was impossible: all eyes were fixed on the native who had just walked into the room, and no one said a word. He realized that these men were not used to seeing an *indio* in a university.

Constantino paid little attention to the other students. He was much too excited about all that he was learning. He treasured every history book he encountered; to him they were doors that opened to reveal all the answers to questions he had been asking his entire life.

His favorite class was government. He learned about the Bolivian Constitution, with its guarantee of inalienable rights for every citizen regardless of race. Bolivia, like other South American countries founded in the wake of the French Revolution, needed to enshrine its protections in law. This also extended to his fellow natives; they were even granted the right to vote in 1952.

So, Constantino thought, *the problem lies in the minds of the people.* The natives were conditioned to think that they weren't worthy of rights, while the whites were conditioned to believe themselves a superior race. But natives *had* rights! They just didn't exercise them! How could they, when over 90 percent of them couldn't even read or speak proper Spanish? Constantino rubbed his chin and thought about this problem. After a while he snapped his fingers and stood up. *Natives are by far the majority of the population!* There was so much work to be done. He felt a burning desire to spend all his energy liberating his people.

Eventually, and much to Constantino's delight, other *indios* began joining him in class. Soon they were working together on every assignment. Everyone, especially the professors, noticed that their grades were consistently higher than those of other students. It was obvious they were hungry to learn.

Constantino and his friends became more and more confident in themselves. They even nominated themselves for student government—despite being ridiculed by the rest of the students.

The native students went everywhere together. They would discuss what they learned in class to others, and encourage more *indios* to go to school. They called themselves the "Movimiento Universitario."

By 1960, Constantino and his companions had already been arrested several times for disturbing the peace. The "Movimiento Universitario" now had 22 members, and they decided to announce themselves with a newspaper article: "The Clock of Time." It was their political manifesto. In it, Constantino argued that neither the right nor the left elements of Bolivia's government were suited to fit the needs of the natives. He proposed the foundation of a new party, the PAN (Political Agrarian Party). With this manifesto, Constantino and his fellow native activists laid the foundation for what would become the motto of "El Indianismo:" It is the *indios*—who toil in the fields and the mines, and go to war to defend the nation—who know what is best for themselves and they should be represented in the government.

Under the banner of the PAN, a fully organized native political party first emerged in Bolivia. They had no financial support, but that didn't stop them from devoting all their energy to a single goal: to win elected seats in Congress.

The response to their political action was typical: they were mocked and harassed. When Constantino and his friends would try to organize natives, they would be arrested by the police and held for a few days before being released. No one took them seriously yet.

III

LOVE & PRISON

A few more years went by. Constantino was getting further involved in the natives' struggle. During this time, Constantino's life took a turn when he met a young woman.

He had noticed her before, on the street where he worked. Every morning he saw her sweeping the entryway of her house. She had long, curly, dark brown hair, bundled up in a ponytail. Her skin was pearly white, like a *patron's*. She badly needed new clothes; whenever Constantino saw her, she was wearing the same dusty, oversized apron. One morning, their eyes finally met. The first thing Constantino noticed was how very *sad* she looked. Her big, brown eyes were swollen with tears, and in attempting to wipe the tears away, she had covered her cheeks in dirt.

He waved at her and said, "Hello," hoping to cheer her up. She gently smiled back.

A few days later, Constantino saw her sitting on the sidewalk and hurried to sit by her—he wanted to learn more about her. Her name was Marie. She'd been orphaned at nine years old and had lived in the streets before finding work as a housekeeper. This was where Constantino presently found her. They agreed to meet again.

Before long, they had fallen in love. Constantino had qualities that Marie admired very much. He was well-educated and driven, but most importantly, he was respectful and sweet to her. They married in 1963.

By this time, Constantino shared his house with his brother David and his family, as well as Manuel. Marie was to live there with him, and she was very excited to finally have a home!

Once they settled in Constantino's house they both noticed that there were many differences that they needed to work on. The lifestyle of a Seventh Day Adventist was new to her. Prayer was said before every meal, and in the morning and evening. Material things were shunned in favor of seeking the Kingdom of God. Marie felt like she was on another planet. Until then, the only life she knew was on the streets where she was free like a bird, with no rules of any kind. Her favorite place—the closest thing she had to home—was an abandoned car with no wheels. Her favorite hobby was to get ahold of any empty carton box, go up the steep hills of the city, and slide along with other children of the streets, screaming their lungs out from all the fun.

Because of this, their marriage involved a lot of conflict. Marie did not have the least idea about cooking. She would burn the food every single day. Not only that, everything else she did around the house was wrong: as an orphan, she didn't learn any domestic skills. At church she could barely stay seated. She had no idea what the pastor was talking about. She would look at the Bible, desperately trying to read, but she had never learned how. The only thing she understood was that she believed in God, to whom she prayed and called "*Papito Rey.*"

But those were the little difficulties. Eventually, and with much patience (although sometimes he would pull his own hair), Constantino was able to teach her some of his cooking skills and other household chores.

The real troubles were outside of their home, where society would not accept a white woman married to an *indio*. Constantino and Marie would overhear all types of terribly ugly comments—even criticism because he was a lot older than her. This would affect them both. Many times their days ended with long arguments.

In the midst of this hostile atmosphere, Constantino continued with his passion for politics and went on with his higher level of education.

Another political movement Constantino was involved with was "MUJA" (*Moviemiento Unido Julian Apaza*), which honored Tupac Katari by his birth name. At this point, in 1964, government authorities arrested him and took him prisoner for a long two years. But even in prison, Constantino never grew tired of reading more books and working to improve himself. Any detail about his ancestors was important. One night, he fell asleep with one of these books on his face.

He had the most vivid dream:

He saw his native people coming from north, south, east, and west. They came at the same time—to the rhythm of drums, in their full splendor, with the colorful clothing that defined them so well. Each group was a little different: some came from the valleys, others from the mountains. Still others emerged from the hot Amazon, or blended with the black race of Yungas. They were all dancing. As they got closer, the drums got louder and louder; suddenly a huge army came from within them! There were thousands of men. Most were on foot, but a few rode ahead of them on horseback. He immediately recognized the man who was leading. It was Tupac Katari himself! And he passed, followed by all his troops, as loud as thunder! With one hand firm he held the reins to his horse, and with the other he waved a flag. Then it became blurry, and the great army all vanished at once. When Constantino woke up, he went over every detail of his dream. The flag held his attention—the *Wiphala*, the flag of his ancestors. He couldn't remember any details, but he also couldn't stop thinking about it.

When he got out of jail the *Wiphala* became an obsession. He felt this was key for his people to reconnect with their identity. He went to all the libraries that he knew, to newspapers, and even old churches, but years went by before he finally found it. He ended up borrowing a personal book from a Peruvian merchant for only one night—but reading the entire thing in one night was no problem for Constantino. It was enough time to recreate a full, detailed, and colored drawing of this authentic native flag.

The *Wiphala*, at last! He couldn't wait to show it to his friends, so he immediately called them to a meeting. They gathered around him to hear what he had to say.

"Brothers: I recreated our ancestors' original flag! Look! Isn't it beautiful?" he said as he unraveled it with a huge smile. "I want to show this to all our people as a symbol of our existence! Of what we used to be, and still are. We have forgotten our history!"

But, to his dismay, the other natives didn't really seem convinced that this was of great importance. They seemed confused.

Julio, one of his friends, scratched his head and asked, "A symbol? It's nice...the idea is nice, but how can it help us? We can try and see what our people think about it."

Then they all left.

A little discouraged, Constantino took his drawing back home. But he still couldn't shake the idea from his head, and it lingered until he finally decided to make a replica of his *Wiphala*. He went to the finest stores, bought the shiniest materials, cut perfect squares of all colors for both sides, and sewed it all together. He would unfurl it all the time just to admire it, thinking about his hero Tupac Katari.

Eventually his excitement passed on to his brothers and in 1970, at the inauguration of the school year, the *Wiphala* was flown beside the Bolivian flag—for the first time after almost two centuries—in Rosario! Constantino had earned great respect from his people.

By this time Constantino had three little daughters who accompanied him, together with his wife. In Rosario he gave a speech about the *Wiphala*. He noticed many natives crying together with him, embracing one another, all hoping that one day they could have a better future. This new hope gave strength and courage to Constantino, and he was overwhelmed with excitement!

Constantino spoke about the struggle of the natives a second time, and on this occasion the newspapers published an article saying that the peasants had used a foreign flag! Constantino and his native brothers thought, "How ironic, now we are the foreigners!" Then, on November of the same year, he gave a speech in front of 30,000 people at Ayo Ayo, along with his fellow students.

Constantino knew that all the attention and the crowds meant that the government would react at some point—but then, he also knew that he needed to be courageous, and so he walked firmly toward the stage and he gave one of the greatest speeches of his life. Holding the flag, he looked at everyone around and asked, "What are we?...*Worms?* Everywhere I turn I see my brothers suffer! We are controlled by foreigners that humiliate us! We are all poor, hopeless, and ignorant! Even the laws are imported, they are not made to fit us. The Right, the Left, they don't care about us, because the ones in control made the system for themselves. They don't understand our position: therefore, the only ones who can change things in our favor are ourselves!

"We need many teachers! Teachers and schools in every town! Every child must study...Those that have a chance to go to school now must go and learn. When you come back, become a teacher!

"We are the only ones that can make a change in our lives! We must realign our minds to a new way of thinking. We can do anything if we really try, but we must do *something!*" He clenched his fists and lifted his arms, looking anxiously at his people. Then he continued.

"I cannot just stay still whenever I see an injustice to our people. Even if they keep arresting me! But if we are not part of the solution, what are we?"

Then he lowered his head, and with both hands tightly against his chest, he went on.

"I feel the screaming of a million natives in my heart, the rumbling of the mountains shaking with pain and anger, saying, '*No more!*' and it's this knot in my throat that doesn't leave me! You know what it is? It's the cry for justice! After years of humiliation, and unpaid punishment of so many massacres, and unlimited abuse! We lost thousands of native brothers in the farms and the silver mines. Nobody answers to us about them. Some generations have gone by, and we got used to this! But this is not how it should be! We deserve better! Today I want to remind you all who we really are. We are descendants of the great Inca Empire. We deserve a better life than what we have today. Brothers, help me to fight for our unalienable rights of life, liberty, and the pursuit of happiness—though they are all in the Bolivian Constitution, as *indios*, we are deprived of them and not even represented in our own government! Most of us are not even conscious that these rights exist! We need to have *indios* in Congress! We must do this, even if it will cost us our lives! It won't be easy. The *patrones* underestimate us. They will surely use violence to stop us. But only we can stand up for us, nobody else cares! Join me when I say: 'Glory to Tupac Katari!'"

The crowd roared. "*Glory!*"

They cheered and applauded as he went on.

"I am thankful that Bolivia became independent from the Spanish Crown. That is a good thing for us too. Remember the war for the lands of Chaco Boreal. The Criollos needed all Bolivians, including us, to fight in that war; as a result we earned more civil rights. And now we have the universal vote! All this means that we have the same rights as every Bolivian! Glory to our Liberators!"

"*Glory!*"

"Another of our biggest problems lies with us. What happened to US? I'm tired of seeing my brothers' defeated faces! Why does it have to be this way?

"Every time we get called *indio* we lower our heads! Are we embarrassed of who we are? Be no more! White people are just another color. There isn't anything that we cannot do just as well as them—or even better! I want to see change! For the next time they call anyone of us *indio* in that despicable way, we must stand tall, look them firmly in their eyes, and say, 'I am *indio*, and proud to be one!'"

At this point something amazing happened. Other natives started taking out *Wiphalas* of their own! He realized that the flag had not been forgotten—perhaps it had always been there. His heart started beating faster. He felt like people were waking up. They looked to one another, holding their heads high, arms stretched to the sky, their eyes determined.

Inspired by Constantino's words, many *indio* children enrolled in schools and colleges. There really was a social movement going on.

As Constantino and his movement's popularity grew, those in power began to pay more attention to him.

Bolivia had been going through a lot of political chaos. The last elected president had been replaced by a string of military dictatorships.

The struggle for Constantino and his *indio* movement would be far harder than they anticipated. Former presidents didn't pay much attention to the *indios*, but soon one of them would. The militia had control of the streets. Order was being forcibly imposed. Eventually, they went after the MUJA. They had enough clues about who Constantino was and where he lived. Rumors were flying about his friends being persecuted. The militia didn't spare women or children.

One night, desperate knocks at Constantino's house woke up everyone. When he opened the door, he saw a native brother, who was pale and panting. The man ran into the house and quickly closed the door behind him.

"Constantino," he managed to say, his words stumbling over each other, "run for your life! Some military agents are coming to arrest you. They know where you live! Go! Save yourself!"

Constantino was startled. He looked at his family, and for one moment he thought, *This is it, the war has begun for me.* Then he turned directly to his daughters and choked for a moment. There was no time to cry, he needed to react quickly!

He turned to his brother. "David, I leave my family to you."

He grabbed a coat and some money and looked to the roofs: this was his only chance of escape. Then he disappeared, like a cat, into the night.

This same moment, the agents arrived. They were banging on the door so loudly it was almost unbearable. David hurried to open the door and let them in. After pushing David around and threatening him, they looked in every room, under the beds, inside the closets, top to bottom, until they were sure that he wasn't there. Then they left, bellowing, "We will find him!"

Constantino disappeared for a while. First he took cover in nearby villages with fellow natives, but it wasn't easy asking for help. Eventually, he ended up hiding in the mountains, where there is a place called "Ciudad de Piedra" ("Stone City"). It is a geological zone filled with enormous rocks from an ancient volcanic eruption. These rocks resemble cement buildings, which is where the name comes from. It was close to Rosario.

He could reach out to his friends there, and the rocks made it a great hiding place.

Some time went by and desperation soon started kicking in. He needed to see his family. He had to find ways to visit home.

IV

THROUGH
THE DARKNESS

Constantino was able to go to his house and see his family a few times without being caught. One night, when his wife was out of town, he cuddled beside his three daughters and all were asleep. Suddenly, the scariest loud banging came from the front door. It was so strong that the door was destroyed in no time; Constantino was not even able to put his pants on. Five or six military men, armored head to toe with black woolen hats that completely covered their faces, had entered his home. They looked ready to destroy anything they came across.

Scared to death, his three little girls ran under the bed. Constantino quickly made signs for them not to move. There they stayed, holding back their tears, almost choking and frightened beyond description. All three looked at their father, horrified, as these strangers surrounded him and started to beat him up. When the punches and kicks came, the girls couldn't make a sound. As Constantino was getting beaten up, he didn't try to defend himself. There was no chance to get away this time. Then the men dragged him to the patio. He saw that his father Manuel was also being beaten by the soldiers. Constantino knew that the rest of his family was in terrible danger—just the thought that his daughters were under the bed scared him more than anything in the world. He knew that it was only a matter of time until they found them, so he quickly followed orders from these men. He was eager to get them to leave. When they finally left with him, he was placed under arrest.

Constantino was taken in a Jeep; one of the soldiers knocked him out with his gun. He was blindfolded and taken to an empty building somewhere in La Paz.

The guards pushed him up the stairs to the second level and uncovered his eyes. He took a quick glance and looked around him. The place was full of offices. It seemed to be some kind of government headquarters.

Constantino asked them, "Why am I here? What are the charges against me?"

But the guards didn't answer. Instead they pushed him more and began to beat him up again. They kicked and punched him everywhere. His hands were cuffed and as soon as he would fall, the men would lift him up again and continue to punch as hard as they could. They exhausted themselves and eventually had to stop, but by the time they were finished, there wasn't a spot that they had missed. He had two broken ribs, his back teeth were gone, and he was throwing up a lot of blood. At some moments he thought he was unable to breath, that he would drown in his own blood. Then one of the soldiers asked:

"What are your plans?"

"What do you think that you can get by stirring up the *indios*?"

"Say it! Are you trying to plot a coup against the president?!"

"Because of you there are so many *indios* rioting everywhere, with that flag that of yours! Are you trying to change our flag?! You are a traitor to this country!"

Constantino replied, "The *Wiphala* belonged to the Incas. To us, it is simply a reminder of our identity—an emblem of our ancestors. That's all."

"A 'reminder of your identity?' Who cares anyway! You're nothing but a stupid *indio*! Do you understand?"

While he said this, he punched Constantino's face again, throwing him to the floor.

Constantino couldn't answer any further. He wasn't moving at all.

The guards thought that he might be dead, and poured cold water over his body. When they noticed that he started shivering, they decided to leave. As they walked away from him, Constantino said, "We want to be able to decide our own destiny, we want to be part of the government, and be treated as equals!"

When they heard this they became enraged. They came back, and this time they dragged his father Manuel with them. One of the guards had him by the hair, forcing him to look at Constantino as he yelled, "*Take a good look, old man, for you will not see him alive again!*" Then he laughed hysterically. At this point Constantino's eyes locked with his father's. Manuel was also badly beaten. There was no light in his eyes. He tried to stay calm. He needed to be there for Constantino somehow, and he wanted him to know how proud he was of him, and

from the bottom of his heart he gained strength to shout, "God
is with you, my son! You are a righteous man!"

Then the guards pushed Manuel down the stairs. Another
one of the men came with a big rock and hit Constantino on
his knee. This was probably the most excruciating pain he ever
felt. When the rock struck his knee, he remembered the day
at the *mercado*, the pain and anger of not being able to defend
his mother then, and now the pain of seeing his father being
tortured for his sake. It hurt so deep, all the way to his heart.
From that moment on his heartbeat was all he could hear.
It was as if his spirit had left his body. He saw himself being
dragged by the soldiers down the stairs and pushed into the
back of a car. They travelled all night.

The soldiers left Constantino at an isolated prison, deep
in the Andes. He was taken to the highest tower, where the
window and door were sets of rusty metal bars, with nothing
to shield him from the elements. The outer part of the prison
was made of thick walls of bricks and cement, but in the cell
blocks, everything was made of mud and dry hay. There was
no floor, only gravel. The bathrooms were pure cement with
septic holes for toilets. There was no running water to flush.
There wasn't even toilet paper.

Constantino was left to the freezing night. He imagined
voices all around him. Some sounded like gruesome laughter,
telling him how stupid he was. Some were from his own people, telling him to stop, that they were better without him. As
his heart grew weaker, he heard one of the voices ask, "What
can you do? Nothing! You are probably crippled by now! Even
if you did survive, you are a broken man! It's better to die now.
All this terrible pain will end, just let go..."

Three days had passed, or maybe more. A female officer was guarding Constantino's cell. While she lit a cigarette, she kept looking at Constantino, wondering if he'd ever get up. She asked another guard as he passed beside her, "Who is this man? What did he do?"

The guard replied, "Ahh! He's just a stupid *indio* stirring up riots, claiming he's doing it for native rights! He is a fool! He says that the *indios* are the rightful owners of this land! I heard that he wants to create a political movement! I wonder if he actually believes that *indios* can get into the government." He shook his head as he walked away, laughing.

But the female guard looked sadly at Constantino and thought, *He really dreams big, and he believes that we deserve better*—for she had *indio* blood herself.

Another day went by and the guard still couldn't stop admiring Constantino's courage. She gently pushed her food against his face and said, "Wake up! You need to eat."

But he would not move. There were times when his body would shiver, but he wouldn't regain consciousness. He continued having nightmares. Finally, they gave way to better dreams. He dreamt of his parents. They were both beside his bed, and they hugged him. He heard his father gently say, "God is with you, my son. Remember your purpose in life. Don't give up! wake up..." And he opened his eyes.

Constantino had actually been hearing the guard's voice, but it was like echoes. Was he dead? He thought, *What is going on? Who are you?* He asked very confusedly, "Are you my friend?" He tried to look at her, but the sunlight was too bright. He tried to move, but he couldn't. His body was too weak.

Constantino had no idea how long he had been unconscious. He turned his face away from the food; he didn't think that he could swallow a thing. But then he mumbled something, and the guard immediately got closer to hear what he was saying:

"Cig...," and he mumbled something else. The guard tilted her face, trying to read his lips, leaning closer to Constantino.

"What is it, my friend?"

"Ciga...rrete...ple...ase...I'm free...zing."

The guard smiled, and quickly lit a cigarette for him. "It's a miracle! You are alive!...You are a very strong man," she said with admiration.

Constantino looked despondent. "What good am I now? Look at me, I'm a mess! Who are you? Why do you care about me?"

The guard covered him with a small blanket and said, "I heard about you. You are a good man. You are trying to make a difference for the natives, but you need to finish what you started. Please don't give up, or all this pain will be for nothing! Your people have their hopes in you! Even I believe in you, Constantino. Eat, please!"

Without realizing it, the guard was encouraging Constantino. She was giving him strength! To Constantino, her voice was like that of his father, telling him to get up, that he was right, and that he was one of the few chosen among his people to take action for justice and equality in Bolivia. He couldn't retreat now! And so, he regained his willpower. He wanted to live! To see his family again! Even though he felt unable to swallow, he found himself commanding his body: "Eat!" "Drink!" "Breathe!" "Sit!" "Get up!" "No excuses! You are a warrior!" "Beat faster!" "Now slowly!" "*You are in control!*"

His healing had begun.

He soon joined the other prisoners. He made new friends—many had heard of him and admired him, and he found many helping hands among all the prisoners. All of them were natives, imprisoned with or without good reason. There were many like Constantino that were arrested for activism. He even found natives that he already knew. Soon everyone in the prison seemed to know who Constantino was, and they all admired his courage. They would carry him around when he couldn't walk, and help him with his basic personal needs. He was even fed by his new friends, until almost all his wounds were healed. Only his knee still felt sensitive.

Eventually Constantino was transferred to La Paz city, where his family could visit him regularly. This prison was much better; it was warmer and there was running water. Every cell was small and made of cement and gravel, but it was clean.

One night something very strange happened. Constantino was abruptly awakened by the guards. They ordered him to dress up and go with them. As usual, he was blindfolded.

He was shoved into a military Jeep. They drove to an abandoned street. Then all the men got off, dragging Constantino with them. When his eyes were uncovered, he saw he was in a lonely, distant place. There were only a few lights far away; it was hard to see anything. The men uncuffed him and then one hollered, "Constantino, you are free! Get out of here!"

Constantino froze for a few seconds. He realized that they were planning to kill him, framing him for trying to escape. He couldn't lift his head and he thought, *This is it, I'm a dead man! Nowhere to run, nothing to do! God help me!* He looked at the floor, his eyes filling with burning tears. There were a few moments of stunned silence. Then he remembered the question the guard had asked: Why did he survive, if it was his time to die anyway? It didn't make sense...*There's got to be more than this, it just can't be over!* He took a deep breath, and slowly picked up his shoulders. Even though his head was still so heavy, he turned toward the vehicle and started to walk. His eyes almost closed; he was ready to hear the crack of the rifle. He muttered to the men, "If you are going to kill me, it will have to be right here, on government property! *You damned cowards!*" Then he got in the Jeep. He had become fearless after all.

The men were confused. This was the last thing that they expected. They slowly looked at one another. Their leader talked over the Jeep's radio, saying that the plan was negative. Then somebody in other end of the radio yelled, "Who ordered you to kill Constantino? Bring him back, you idiots!" Their new orders were to take Constantino to another one of the government headquarters, "DOP," where he was tortured. The excuse for these tortures was always that he had committed treason, but in reality, it was just hate. The mocking was clear and direct. They wanted to trample him like a cockroach. After that he was taken back to the prison.

The days went on and sometimes it was harder for Constantino to be strong. His relationship with his wife had worsened. She gave in to depression. Many times, she would beg him to forget about politics. It was very hard for her to understand his situation. She was a simple woman whose greatest aspiration was to have a family like any other. She asked herself, *What could be so powerful that a man would put aside his own family to follow it?* She also felt caught between the crossfire of the *indios* and the white people. When she visited him in prison, the other prisoners would shout and ask her why she was there, a white woman in an *indios* jail. This was breaking her as well as Constantino. Every time she visited him they would argue. Things got so out of control that finally they decided to get divorced. Since the house belonged only to him, it was Marie who had to leave, and the girls would have to stay under the supervision of their Uncle David.

Constantino's father had died while he was in jail. He never got to say goodbye. Pain after pain! It seemed that his world was crumbling down on him. But he was able to get up every day when he imagined holding his daughters again.

One day he noticed that many natives would come to the door of the penitentiary. They would ask about him every day, a couple of times even by the hundreds. Knowing that his people cared about him encouraged Constantino greatly, though this naturally made the authorities uncomfortable.

They didn't have any official charges against Constantino. People would ask questions about his case that had no answers.

On August 1st of every year Bolivia celebrates *Dia del Indio*, the Day of the Natives. It is a good opportunity for both sides to talk about mutual interests.

In 1974, as usual, they called to an assembly at one of their headquarters, the "Ministerio de Asuntos Campesinos."

Thousands of *indios* were there, lining all the streets, around all the government offices, anxious to know: what was the gift for them this year?

A government representative went out to the balcony, where he gave a speech appropriate for the day. As he honored the native people, he asked what it was that they would like for this day. Somebody yelled as loud as he could, "Free Constantino! He's an innocent brother!" When the rest of the natives heard this, they all started yelling the same thing. It became louder and louder. "*Free Constantino! Free Constantino!*"

The Governor looked puzzled for a moment. This request was a surprise. He didn't know who this Constantino was! Perhaps it was somebody remarkable...*No*, he thought, *it must not be anybody important*—for he had not heard of him. But it looked like all the *indios* cared, so, for now, his only option was to say anything to calm them down. He offered to take a close look into Constantino's case, and agreed to meet with everyone the next day in the same place. He realized that he would have to deliver Constantino back to his people.

The governor was under tremendous pressure: on one hand, his superiors, and on the other hand, all the natives...

Early next morning at the penitentiary, Constantino was ordered to get cleaned up and dressed to meet with the governor.

As soon as he was escorted into the governor's office, Constantino could sense that something was about to happen, and he was ready.

"So you are the famous Constantino!"

"Yes."

"I've received orders to set you free, under certain restrictions. You are not to become involved in any type of political activity or social movements of any kind. You are banned from La Paz city, under the punishment of imprisonment if you return. You must sign this document of agreement, and then you are free."

Constantino thought, *Freedom! I can go home, live my life, be with my family! Not a bad deal at all...But what about everyone else! My native brothers, they believe in me. They are counting on me! Now I have a purpose in life! I could not look at myself in the mirror if I turn away from them now!*

Constantino turned his face to the man. "What is freedom, governor? Are you proposing a half freedom? I'm free, but I'm not?

"No thanks. If I've done wrong, I'm punished. If not, I'm free. Simple as that. You can put me back in jail, because if you set me free, I will fight for my people's rights until my last breath!"

And as he said this he offered his hands for the governor to put his cuffs back on.

The governor rubbed his head. This man was determined indeed! And just outside the doors of the palace were all the natives waiting for Constantino. He felt defeated, and at the same time he felt admiration for Constantino. Without further ado, he signed the release documents. Constantino was free at last!

There was a great ovation. Surrounded by the love of his native brothers, Constantino was escorted all the way to his house.

David was at the door. He hugged Constantino tight; both men cried. David explained how their father Manuel never recovered from the beating. This felt like a knife in Constantino's heart. It was because of him that Manuel died! David told Constantino that the situation with his daughters was very difficult. The girls tried to escape a couple of times in search of their mother, and at one point they succeeded. Luckily, they had returned, although they never explained why. As Constantino was holding his head in his hands, imagining his little girls out in the streets by themselves, they ran into the house. The girls jumped on top of him and showered him with kisses. Their smile and their laughter would sustain him; they would not let him fall apart. David had taken good care of them. This meant so much to Constantino. He dried his tears. Their love was God's cornerstone for him! More than enough to keep him strong! That night he sang to his daughters a few songs that he wrote himself, over and over with his *zamponia* (native musical instrument), until they fell asleep. When he was alone later that night, he cried once more. His heart was so heavy that the pain was almost unbearable. The love he had for his wife, even now, made him hurt so deeply. He walked to the patio of his house, looking to the skies, searching for answers. His knees were shaking, and it was hard to stand. David—who also couldn't sleep—stood beside him, repeating Psalms 23:4: "Even though I walk through the valley of the shadow of death, I will fear no evil: for Thou art with me: Thy rod and Thy staff they comfort me."

V

A GLOBAL PEOPLE'S MOVEMENT

In the months after his release, Constantino became more active than ever. Even though Bolivia was still under a dictatorial regime, there were international entities that contacted the MUJA. one of them was from Canada, another country that stands out for its large indigenous population.

All the way on Vancouver Island was Mr. George Manuel, the most important native figure from the Canadian west coast. He was chief of the Assembly of First Nations, and the founder and president of the World Council of Indigenous Peoples.

George Manuel prepared to hold the largest international conference of indigenous people at the island. He invited native leaders from all around the world. This invitation was also sent to Bolivia, to the office of MUJA, whose leader at that time was Julio Tumiri. In addition to another delegate, he suggested including Constantino; the three of them would represent Bolivia.

All of this happened fast. Constantino was very excited! He was going to meet with his brothers from all around the world! He kept wondering what he was going to say. These were all the great native leaders—he had a lot to learn from them too!

The day came when he boarded the plane to Canada. He wished his father were alive to witness all that he was about to accomplish. Then he sat back to prepare himself for this special event.

Once they arrived in Canada, they had guides and interpreters who took all travelers to the island.

The next day, the meetings took place.

And there they were, all in their native clothing, full of all the colors of Mother Nature. One by one, Constantino looked over them all with admiration. It sure was a delight to his eyes!

Then came all the dances! It was amazing! Every place with their own culture: Argentina, Australia, Bolivia, Canada, Colombia, Ecuador, Finland, Greenland, Guatemala, Mexico, New Zealand, Nicaragua, Norway, Panama, Paraguay, Peru, Sweden, the United States, and Venezuela.

As the native leaders discussed each country's situation, it was clear that their problems were very similar. Constantino's turn came, and he gave a great speech, as usual. Now, the world would hear the reality of the Bolivian natives as well.

He built good friendships with a group from Port Alberni, where the World Council of Indigenous People was being held. He also met with many white people who supported equality; this made him feel a very special and warm comfort. Denny and Sara Durocher (the main reason for their presence at the beginning was to translate Spanish to English); Ron Hamilton,

Constantino at the First Wold Council of Indigenous People

an important Canadian native artist; and especially George Watts, who was manager for the Tseshaht Band of the Nuu-chah-nulth people at that time. From the beginning, there was a connection between Constantino and George. With the help of Sara Durocher, they became best friends by the end of the first day. The purpose of the WCIP was to establish concepts of aboriginal rights on a worldwide scale. The delegates were to attend five workshops about important indigenous issues:

1. Have representation at the United Nations. (*This would mean that the world would know all about the Indian peoples' problems! He was overwhelmed with excitement!*)
2. Create a Charter for themselves
3. Social, economic, and political justice
4. Retention of cultural identity
5. Retention of land and natural resources.

Constantino and his *indio* brothers had to pinch each other to make sure that this was not a dream.

The days went by very quickly. He made so many friends, he couldn't keep track. But time was running out.

About three days before returning to Bolivia, Constantino and his friends were sharing a dinner.

He and George were having a very deep conversation. Constantino had been doing a lot of thinking, and felt that he could talk with George about almost anything.

George was a Canadian native, who was doing well in life and had an earned a very nice position among his own people in Vancouver. It felt like they had known each other before, and the words were shared easily between the two.

George saw in Constantino a man who suffered so much, and yet would not bow to anyone that disrespected him. He was always ready to say what he felt was right. His courage made him stand out wherever he went; despite his small size and his humble clothing, he spoke loud, clear, and firm about his beliefs.

Constantino felt that this was an opportunity to take care of one of his greatest concerns, and knew that he needed to act immediately, so he went straight to the point...

The moment came when George asked, "My friend, Constantino, is there anything I can do to help you?"

This was the moment that he had been waiting for!

"Yes!" Constantino answered, as his eyes filled with tears. "I have three daughters, who are possibly in danger, and my enemies might try to take them from me. It is impossible to work for my people while I am worried about them. I wish they were safe."

George's eyes seemed bigger than ever as he looked at Constantino. Was he asking him to take his daughters to Canada?

Constantino's eyes said it all! That was exactly what he meant!

George suddenly realized the magnitude of this request— what this meant—and he was overcome with emotion. He didn't have any children yet, he thought to himself, and in a split second, he imagined himself, his wife, and three girls! What a request! He took a deep, deep breath, and said... "Yes! I will take your daughters. I will raise them like my own, for as long as you need. I will care for them and make sure that they are never lonely!

"My friend, and now my brother, don't worry anymore. We shall prepare all documents needed. Go in peace."

So when Constantino returned to Bolivia, it seemed that the days were numbered: he barely had enough time to arrange his daughters' trip to Canada. Student visas were granted immediately.

Among his political followers, he had recently met a new lady. This woman was native like him, with the same ideals and goals. She was very determined and strong-minded, a warrior that would stand strong beside him. They got married right away and soon became a great couple. He was very happy to have someone again.

The time came to send his daughters to Canada.

One day he sat down with them and went over everything about their trip.

Constantino's excitement about his goals in life often made him lose focus and connection with his girls. He never asked them about how they felt. Deep inside, whenever he looked into their eyes, he knew that it was better not to ask. He knew that they had too many questions; he knew that very quietly they would gather in their bedroom to cry for their mom.

Even though they did not really understand what was happening, the girls had to trust any decision from their father. So they left with two of Constantino's good friends from Canada.

VI

FINAL IMPRISONMENT AND FREEDOM

Soon after that, in June 1976, Constantino was imprisoned yet again.

This time the physical ordeal was worse, and much more humiliating. He was tortured again and again. His torturers didn't think he was really a threat. They probably realized that Constantino didn't stand a chance against any political forces, much less the national army. In fact, he didn't stand for any political party at all. So they made up the excuse that he was a traitor. At one point his mouth was propped open with a nail and he was forced to eat human feces. His head was plunged into the toilet, then he was thrown into the dungeon again.

For many months his family and friends had no clue about him. This time his people didn't know where to look for him. They couldn't find a way to help Constantino. He was shattered, each day wondering if this was his last. Many months passed before his family was able to see him again. The visits were very limited. Sometimes his wife and David had to wait hours to spend only a few minutes visiting Constantino. But every moment was used well. Constantino was a man who was able to control his emotions. Instead of pitying himself, he always thought with clarity and never gave up hope. Through his wife, he sent many letters to his daughters and friends in Canada. He was able to write a very touching letter, humbly pleading for himself and family. He ended the letter by signing, "May God repay you all."

When this letter was received by his Canadian friends, they made hundreds of copies and sent them to everyone that had heard of Constantino.

His friends in Canada got together on a regular basis to talk about him and his family, as a way to cheer up his daughters. A new addition to the group, Mike Lewis, suggested getting the church involved and contacting the United Nations. They even came up with the decision to create a name for themselves as a fully organized entity: they would be called "The Aymara Society." They wrote all their letters under this name. Some were sent to the Bolivian government, others to Amnesty International and the National Council of Churches, asking about Constantino's disappearance. The Indigenous Council began to help as well.

There were many witnesses at the time he was arrested, so the Bolivian government couldn't deny that they had him.

Almost a year went by. It was February, 1977.

Inside the prison, Constantino was on the verge of giving up. He had no strength to continue living. He was hopeless, thinking that it might be the end. He thought a lot about his father. He needed him so much.

He had told his wife that he was being tortured on a nearly daily basis. His diet was a tiny portion of only rice, and he shared a cell with six other prisoners.

AYMARA SOCIETY MEMBERS AND FRIENDS

Durocher Family

Darlene Watts

Dr. Gabriel Sevy

George Watts and Simon Lucas

Bob Soderlund   Terry Whyte

Early one morning, the prison guards took Constantino out and into a car. He was sure that they were going to kill him this time. His heart was beating very loudly. He thought, *Nothing can save me. I have already played all my cards.*

His body was so beaten, he could hardly walk. Every step was terribly painful, and he had no chance to defend himself. In his mind he imagined saying his last words to his daughters; even though he tried to hold back his tears, they rolled quietly down his face. This was his second breaking point. What could possibly help him? He lifted his head to the skies and thought about God. "Please, help me," he quietly pleaded. That was when he realized that he was being taken to La Paz city. He wondered what was happening…

Once in La Paz, he was taken to the DOP, where, after waiting four hours, he received an old passport. While he waited in a locked room, he could hear people going in and out and talking a lot, but he couldn't hear what it was about.

Suddenly the door opened and a guard entered—followed by his wife! She was shivering from excitement, but also fear. As the guard left, he said, "You have five minutes."

They hugged and kissed. There was only time for a few words. "I only brought enough clothes for you to change once, I was told you are being exiled!" she said tearfully. "I don't know if I'll ever see you again, or hear about you. I don't know where they are taking you."

"I love you."

And that was all they had time to say.

Then a man that seemed to be higher-ranking came in and said, "You are being exiled to Canada. I don't know what you did, but somehow my superiors singed your release papers and sent me to make sure that you leave Bolivia!"

Then Constantino was escorted to a police car and taken to the airport where he saw two nuns sitting at a coffee table. He was being taken straight toward them! This definitely meant good news!

The guards are delivering me to the nuns, who will take me to safety! Hope filled again in his eyes!

The nuns explained to Constantino that he had been granted political asylum in Canada. He was to land precisely in Vancouver! They handed him an airplane ticket. They were also about to give him 200 American dollars, but a greedy look from one of Constantino's guards discouraged them. The nun put it back in her pocket and eventually forgot to give it to Constantino!

The plane would first take him to Lima, Peru and from there he would connect with Iberia Airlines to Vancouver City. He didn't have a single penny in his pocket, but he was free!

As brave as he was, he could barely cope with everything that was happening. It all felt like a dream, getting on the plane, walking to his seat. Once the plane took flight and reached the clouds, he felt a weight off his shoulders.

Then, as the trip kept going, he started wondering how he was going to contact his friends, trying to remember any details of Vancouver Island. He needed to think, and have a plan...

When the plane arrived in Vancouver, immigration officers questioned Constantino for several hours. They wanted to make sure that he wasn't a threat of any kind. They asked him about his political positions: was he a liberal or a conservative? Was he from the right or the left? The questioning became tiring, until Constantino asked them directly, "What is it that you want from me? Arrest me then, if that is what you want, or leave me to be free! I don't side with the right or the left! I represent the Bolivian native people, and that is all."

After that, he was let go.

After going through immigration, he quickly got a hold of a telephone guide, and started looking for George Watts. As he was doing so, a man tapped him on the back. He must have looked so desperate that even a stranger wanted to help him. The man asked him if he needed anything. Constantino said he was trying to locate George Watts. Remarkably, the man had heard of George Watts! He was even willing to take him to the Island, all the way to Port Alberni! *Surely there is a God!* Constantino thought.

It was a Sunday. Denny and Sara had been spending the weekend with the three Bolivian girls and their own baby, having some family time, when the phone rang.

Sara answered. "Hello? Hi George...What?...*What?*" Oh, God! *Oh my God!*"

Her voice kept getting louder. Immediately the family surrounded her, and as her face turned to joy, her tears and smile said it all. Denny knew right away, and exclaimed, "*Constantino!*"

Sara quickly grabbed a pen and paper and wrote an address with trembling hands. Then she hung up the phone and cheered. "He is here!"

The girls started jumping and hugging each other. Everyone was running around the house to grab a coat, and crammed into the car to go and receive Constantino at last!

After traveling for a couple of hours to a nearby town, the Durochers parked at a gas station. They waited for a yellow Volkswagen, as they were told. Every eye inside Denny's car was set on the Volkswagen's arrival, every breath held in anticipation.

And there it was! The passenger door opened, and Constantino emerged. It was like looking at a ghost. He was thin to the bone, and had a long, long beard. He walked crookedly, almost dragging one of his legs. He was wearing a long, thin, dark green coat. At first it was hard to recognize him, but as he got closer, everyone ran to him. There was so much happiness to be shared, and many, many long hugs. It was one more of those moments in life, that make it worth everything...

In Canada, life was wonderful. Especially in Port Alberni, where everybody seemed to know about Constantino. They loved him and his family. Wherever they went, they were welcomed. The natives and the white folks living there all took care of every need for Constantino. At this point it could have been so easy to forget about Bolivia. To him the island was like a beautiful dream. Enjoying time with the Tseshaht tribe, endless evenings filled with good stories, camping at the beach by the fire with all the delicious salmon cooking, and surrounded by live music, and the enchantments of their dances! What more can a man ask? After a month, even his wife and a tiny new daughter had joined them in Canada!

But Constantino never forgot his heart's calling. He needed to go back. And so he waited, and waited...

It was the middle of 1978, when finally the president of Bolivia called for national elections. At the same time, he declared general amnesty for all political leaders.

The time had come!

Constantino was a lot healthier. He was even slightly over-weight. His strength had been renewed.

The love of his family and friends worked wonders, and with the help of doctors, he made a full recovery.

Constantino with the Haack Family

When he told his daughters that he was going back, he noticed that they were very quiet. They never asked anything; it seemed like they were holding back. There were many things left unsaid. No emotions on the outside, while their hearts were screaming for peace. Children don't understand racism, or politics, white, or *indio*; they just knew that they loved their *indio* father as much as their white mother. Sometimes when he would express his anger toward the Spanish people, he would notice their frightened eyes and he would calm down.

They never dared ask about their mom, even though this situation was really hurting them. *I need to heal and overcome my scars*, he thought to himself. He realized that the "mestizos," like his daughters, were the future; whether anyone liked it or not. And the new generations had no idea about the wrong-doings of the past.

On his flight back to Bolivia, he sat calmly in the plane. This was his victory. He had overcome so many obstacles; he was able to stand up for justice and not be defeated. Even though the road to equality was still very long, he knew that he had come far, and he was eager to continue working for his people. All the horrible things that happened to him were in the past. He felt like he was stepping into a new episode in Bolivian history, one with more clarity, where democracy would be restored and the natives would decide their own destiny.

The End

ABOUT THE AUTHOR

The author's passion for literature started in elementary school. Her favorite books were from C.S. Lewis and Walter Farley. Following their style, she won a couple of contests for story writing in school. Eventually, her interest inclined for Gabriel Garcia Marquez and Eduardo Galeano among her favorites. It has been one of her lifetime dreams to write a book. Her main goal for this book was to put together in simple language a compelling and enjoyable read of a good story. Much of her inspiration happened at Vancouver Island, Canada, where she has many wonderful friends.

About Constantino Lima Chavez

A Bolivian native who at a very young age became an activist for native peoples' rights.

To this day, he is a strong advocate for any injustice toward his people. His work inspired many native Bolivians to overcome oppression.

Unfortunately, the amount of torture and hate towards him from his enemies have caused wounds that will never heal both physically and spiritually.

He received recognition from President Evo Morales in the year 2002 for restructuring the *Wiphala*. He was named Apu Mallku, which means "Great Leader," by his Aymara people.

Very close with another native, he was one of the first natives to represent his people in Bolivia's Congress by the year 1980.

He was also one of the first natives to graduate from Universidad Mayor de San Andres with a master's degree in Law and Political Science.

You're shattered
Like you've never been before
The life you knew
In a thousand pieces on the floor
And words fall short in times like these
When this world drives you to your knees
You think you're never gonna get back
To the you that used to be
Tell your heart to beat again
Close your eyes and breathe it in
Let the shadows fall away
Step into the light of grace
Yesterday's a closing door
You don't live there anymore
Say goodbye to where you've been
And tell your heart to beat again...

~Danny Gokey
(Matthew West, Bernie Herms, Randy Phillips)

Inspired by a true story. Some names have been changed and omitted with respect to privacy.
Special thanks to my dear friends in Port Alberni, British Columbia: Mike Lewis (without his help, it wouldn't have been possible), the Haack family, the Durocher family, George Watts and his family, Anita Watts, and Ron Hamilton.
Special thanks to my friends Juliana Hayes and Patticita, and to my family for all their support.
May God's will be done.